BEEKEEPING FOR BEGINNERS

TABLE OF CONTENTS

INTRODUCTION

Thank you for choosing Beekeeping for Beginners*: All You Need to Know to Raise and Maintain Your First Bee Colonies.*

Most people know of the honeybees, but few of us know much about the beehive, the product of the hive, and the historical reference towards the bees. In reality, honeybees and the stuff they collect have been downgraded or forgotten in agriculture and industrial application as well as salesmanship of the present-day world. The bees to most are more a reflection of little importance. Why? Could all the reference of cultures and tribes, west and east, south and north, from the beginning have all been wrong? No, it is because the industrialized world operates on exclusive or patent ownership of things for profitability.

Anybody can own beehive. It's non-exclusive and non-patentable. Honeybees and their products have been a source of sweetness ever since people discovered them. Initially, people see robbing from the tree, in cave or bees nesting as the only means of gathering honey. This process was too hard on the bees. And it later evolved to people keeping honeybees.

If you are thinking of dabbling into beekeeping as a hobby, this guide is a must-read for you, because you will learn about the honeybee's history, nature, and importance. You will also learn how to establish your own hive, various means of acquiring bees, what is best to feed bees, how to prevent pests and predators, how to harvest honey, and much more.

CHAPTER ONE

Bee's Nature and History

Since Bees can keep a close relationship with humans, their behavior has been well-studied. Honeybees reside in well-structured colonies and don't need hibernation. They are well recognized for their honey production, which they stock inside wax combs in their nests. Bees are naturally active in the spring when they are out searching for plants from which they will receive nectar and pollen. They produce honey from these two ingredients, which mans have harvested for several decades.

Honeybees are known to be social beings, which reside within colonies with a few male drones, thousands of workers, and a queen. Workers make use of wax that they release from their abdominal gland to make a nest. Adolescent workers put nectar and pollen within each cell as food for developing larvae. Male drones are removed from the nest to die in the autumn, having accomplished their sole duty in life, which is mating with queens. Honeybee's age also plays a significant role in knowing which individuals execute different daily activities.

Honeybees are very flexible. They hunt for food en-masse. A colony could live for many years without foraging, feeding on their reserved foods, and huddling in vast compacted multitudes in the winter. Honeybee's behaviors are similar in Europe, Asia, Africa, and other parts of the world. However, some species are more aggressive than others. Just like some insects, bees are very defensive, protecting the entrance to their nest when intruders are coming closer. Although they can only sting one time, since stingers have barbs that are attached to the worker's intestine, after attacking a victim, the barb detached naturally from the stinging bee's body.

Meanwhile, a bee will die shortly after transferring its pheromones secreted; venom in the course of the attack will alert and motivate other worker bees also to attack.

Honeybees are among the most common social insects on earth; they make large colonies that can accommodate up to 80,000 individual insects, reside in hives, and produce honey. They remain the leading pollinating insect in the whole universe and among the most vital links in the entire ecosystem.

Honeybees remain pollinators for over one hundred and thirty agricultural plants, and it is estimated in the United States that they are involved in eighty per cent of the food consumed by Americans. The estimated amount of monetary value honey bees pollination contributes to American crops, and the economy is about sixteen billion dollars.

Honey bees nature also includes:

- They are smaller than other bees and not as hairy as bumblebees. Their bodies are a bit slim and long. They are mostly confused with wasps and hornets due to their similar body structure.

- They live in organized colonies, which are like a caste system. Every bee has its respective roles and responsibilities in keeping up the hive and helping the colony thrive.

- Queen is the mother of them all. It resides in the middle of the hive, lays eggs that form the remaining part of the colony, and rely on the other hive members.

- Drones are male. Their primary assignment is to mate the queen.

- Workers are generally female. They have to forage for nectar, protect the offspring, take care of the larvae, and provide food.

- Honey bees are generally calm and docile. Their main concern in their life cycle is to maintain the colony, not seeking people to sting. The only time they are fatal is when their territory is threatened; this is when they attack the invaders en-masse. They tend to chase their invaders or predators over a long distance.

- The variation between honey bees and other bees, wasps, hornets, and other stinging insects is that they have barbs that are attached to their intestine. After attacking a victim, they naturally detach from the stinging bee's body, which will lead to their death shortly after transferring its pheromones secreted, venom in the course of the attack. In contrast, other stingers could sting as many times as possible.□

- They are vital to the environment, so they are to be protected. A collapse colony could lead to societal menace. If you notice a bee colony being constructed anywhere near your property or house, try to call professionals as using layman remedies may lead to severe issues to the society.

CHAPTER TWO

Honeybees Caste inside the Hive

Colonies of honey bee are well structured, such that each caste has its divided and separate role to play and they are naturally suited to their respective roles.

- **Workers**

Three different castes of honey bees exist in a hive; the densely populated ones are the worker bees. They consist of about eighty-five percent of the colony and responsible for the most physical tasks such as pollen and nectar collection. If you observe honey bees bustling from flower to flower, they are workers and also female. All worker bees are female. It is not as if men are left with no line of duty; they are not just naturally good at anything apart from mating.

Even though worker bees are female, none of them is fertile. They are subjected to pheromones released by the queen that will subdue their capacity to develop a suitable reproductive apparatus. Though, they have the innate ability to lay eggs but not to fertilize them.

Through the summer, a worker bee has about five to six weeks of life expectancy, all of which will be spent engaging in one activity or the other. There are numerous works to be done in the colony, and almost everyone of them ought to be executed by the workers. Instead of allocating particular tasks to particular bees, the colony perfectly splits it up by age. This means a worker bee only performs the duty aligned to her age at a time. Therefore, she is likely to perform every task at some point during her month.□

The Life of a Worker

Each bee starts as an ordinary egg in the usual hexagonal honeycomb cell. A worker egg spends twenty-one days to develop into larvae and then into a wholly developed adult worker. It means a worker bee takes nearly the same time she spends as an adult in developing. As soon as she grows into adulthood, the first task of a worker bee is cleaning up the cell in which she was raised. The cell would now turn into a nursery for a fresh egg.

A worker bee would function as a nurse bee for the first twelve days; she will continue to work with larvae by cleaning their cells, keeping them warm, and feeding them. In her next phase of life, from around twelve to twenty days old, the worker will advance to housekeeping tasks around the hive. In this stage, there are lots to be done – storing pollen and nectar, guarding the entrance, warming the hive when it's too cold, cooling the hive when it's too hot, removing dead bodies, building comb, producing wax and much more. Through both the housekeeping and nurse stages, a worker would also spare her time to serve the queen.

The worker becomes a forager at about twenty days old. A colony needs various supplies from the outside world to survive, and it's the task of foragers to provide them for the colony. The resources to provide are nectar – for making honey, and pollen – primarily for feeding the brood. She might also take back tree resin for making propolis, water for cooling, and drinking. She will continue her foraging until she passes on, around ten days later from exhaustion. She can still fly about five hundred miles before her wings give in, and she would make use of every single one of them. This is the order of stages of a worker bee's life – easy task inside the hive at a young and healthy age and then strenuous jobs outside for as long as she could cope. Though worker bees normally live for about a month, they could live a bit longer in the winter period, when there is excessive cold. At this time, they don't go out foraging, and their primary task is to keep the beehive adequately warm for survival.

The physiological disposition of the worker bee is based on the period of the year, which she exists. Bees born in wintertime are prepared to experience the cold winter month. The worker bees born during autumn could survive all through to the spring. This is very important to the existence of the colony since the production of brood during winter is unreal.

- **The Queen**

The same as the human kingdom, a beehive can only have one queen bee. Though she is not the decision-maker, her brain is smaller than that of the workers. Nevertheless, she's the mother of every single bee in the colony. Therefore, she can influence the mood of the entire hive with her pheromones.

For the beekeepers that set up a package of bees during the spring, interestingly, they will notice that after about two months, almost all the population of the bees would be a new member and not part of the original package apart from the queen.

Queen bee is a female. She is born from the egg as that of the workers. She is fed with royal jelly more than three days during her larval stage. Royal jelly is a smooth goop secreted by the worker bees that have an exclusively high content of sugar. This unique diet and also a bigger birth cell give her the capacity to exude pheromones and makes for her bigger body. She is the only bee that can mate among the larger population of the bee colony. This is considered as her primary assignment in life. Shortly after her birth, she embarks on orienting flight, accompanied by a series of mating flights

These flights seem quite mysterious as they happen as high as a hundred feet in-flight, in the place the bees have agreed upon to meet. Drones assemble in this location and the queen of about a week old will join them. Only because the queen appears does not justify the end of work for the drones. They ought to join up with her mid-flight to mate with the queen. The queen generally mates with about ten to twenty drones in the course of her flights. When she mates, the queen will gather about five million different sperm, stored them in her body, and utilize them to lay fertilized eggs one after the other. This sperm can last her for five years

As soon as the queen has mated, she returns to the beehive, and after three days, she begins laying eggs. Eggs laying now turn out to be her way of life. During spring, when there is an upsurge in their population, she lays through both day and night, be around an egg every twenty seconds. A colony with an early population of about twenty to thirty thousand bees would have grown to about sixty thousand bees later in the year. This comprises of plenty of eggs, and they all descend from a single "queen" bee.

An instance of excessive eggs-laying can result in a swarm. This is not a bad thing to occur, and if you see a colony as a single creature, you will reflect on how it reproduces. If the beehive is becoming congested, for both the queen to lay and the workers to store supplies, the later will begin raising a new queen. Swarm is the sign of a well-growing colony. However, it can, on occasion, be an inconvenience to humans.

Workers will build about twenty queen cells for them to raise a new queen. The queen would lay a fertilized egg in every individual cell, and the workers will raise the larvae on royal jelly. About 9 days to swarm occurrence, the older queen will, for the first time, go out of the hive with half to two-thirds of the workers and a few drones in search of a location for a colony.

Eight days later, in the hive, the first of the new queens emerges from the cell. For what reasons are they raising twenty queens in place only one? The new queen is also wondering. As her duty, the queen moves from one queen cell to another, stinging her still-growing sisters to death. A condition where more queens emerge before the first queen could kill all of them; they will have to battle until only one survives. This is one of the ways to clone a new queen, but not the only means. At times you can experience swarm, not for the reason that the colony is growing well, but because the queen is becoming old and weary. If this occurs, they will perform this same process to produce a new queen. At any time if the queen dies, the workers will scramble to make a new one as soon as possible.

For the first three days, all larvae are fed royal jelly. If there are available larvae under 3 days old, the workers would have to continue feeding them royal jelly and prolong the length of their cell. If there are no larvae under 3 days old, the colony would not be able to clone a queen because the source of royal jelly supplied to the larvae would have been lost.

- **The Drones**

Drones (males) are the final caste. They are merely a small proportion of the population of an average colony, and their primary assignment is to mate. Drones possess big eyes to assist them in locating the queen on a mating flight. However, they don't have foraging tools or stingers.

Some animals could reproduce only from unfertilized eggs once their atmosphere does not permit sexual reproduction. Nevertheless, various classes, such as honey bees only reproduce in this way as a matter of sequence.

Once an unfertilized egg is being laid by the queen, it automatically becomes a drone. This means drones do not have fathers. However, they do have grandfathers – their mother was produced by the stored-up sperm of some long dead and far away drones.

Drones are different from other bees

Drones are created asexually. Their eggs are unfertilized, different from queens and workers. This process is called parthenogenesis, and it occurs in nature over and beyond human imagination. In the course of mating flight way up in the air, a drone that manages to have engagement with the queen does not neatly separate. Once mating is completed, a drone's reproductive tissues are removed and remain in the queen, hence causing drone's death.□

Apart from the fact that drone does not reproduce, his life expectancy is naturally short. If winter is forthcoming or there is a shortage of food, the drones will be the first to leave. Workers send them out of the hive and deny them access to come back. Their chance of surviving outside for an extended period is zero.

CHAPTER THREE

Honeybees Communication and Social Life

- ## The Mystic of Pheromones

The pheromones that bees discharge to influence the conduct of other bees around them represent the ways a colony of hundreds of thousands of individuals relates perfectly together.

Pheromones of honey bee can be divided into two main clusters: releaser and primer.

1. Workers bees release releaser pheromones to respond to particular activities

2. The queen bee release primer pheromones to maintain the social order.

The queen signal is one of the main primer pheromones. It's a unique combination of pheromones, and if it does not present in the colony, there would be no social order. The signal of the queen motivates workers to perform their duty, stops them from laying eggs, and prevents them from raising a new queen

The sign of the queen also has a releaser influence that makes other bees close to her. She uses this on a mating flight to invite drones, to keep the group together during a swarm and assemble workers to groom her. If a queen becomes overly weak or dies, the queen signal is no longer apparent, and workers begin to breed a new queen. Brood produces its own primer pheromone that performs the function of keeping the workers from laying eggs. Because workers can't mate, they could only lay unfertilized male eggs which are not sustainable. ☐

- **Stinger**

The pheromones created by worker bees are releases, using it to respond to certain events that happen to them. A good example is the alarm pheromones that are released when an intruder is being stung by a worker. This alarm pheromone begins discharging the moment the worker is ready to sting; notifying other bees immediately, the needs to defend has arisen. Even after the stinging, the pheromones will continue to discharge from the stinger, fixed in the victim and inviting more bees. That is a good reason to leave the beehive if you are being stung. □

Worker bees also discharge orientation pheromone on first flights to guide themselves back to the hive and at the entering point of the hive to guide other bees to their abode. They will discharge recruitment to mark a location to which they will draw other worker bees.

- **Wiggle/waggle dance**

Dancing is another means by which bees communicate. The dance is displayed by a forager that discovered an exceptional supply of nectar and the dance is marvelously precise.□

To disseminate her enormous discovery, the forager walks straight and figure-eight lines, while shaking her wings. Each part of the dance holds important news that every forager watching understand. The period of the dance signifies the distance of nectar to the hive. Every seventy-five milliseconds add about three hundred and thirty feet to the distance.

The extent of the dance signifies the abundance of the source of nectar. An intense waggle means an enormous quantity of nectar.

The most exciting aspect of the waggle dance is that the forager indicates the route to the nectar by showing where it is, in relation to the sunlight. If the nectar is precisely in the direction of the sunlight's present location, the forager will dance in a straight path up the dance floor. If it is around eighty degrees to the left–side of the sun, she will demonstrate eighty degrees straight up to the left side. The bees understand it, and they will fly in the appropriate direction to acquire the nectar.□

CHAPTER FOUR

Importance of Honeybees

The position of honeybees in the human race is important beyond our understanding. The small insect that works quietly and so tirelesly in our environments is undoubtedly one of the reasons, if not the main reason, for the likelihood of human development on the earth surface. Without their existence, the development of human life on earth wouldn't have been the same and the condition of development of human might not have been better. Human beings, the flowers, the bees and all other things that developed alongside humans are all interrelated sequence of occurrences over a remarkable period.

In the artwork, writings and symbolism of religions and cultures across the globe, from time immemorial are references to the honey bees, the stuff they collect and produce from them, such as wax, royal jelly, bee propolis, bee pollen, and honey. These substances, together with beehive and bees, are attached with great significances through human history all over the world. The references are mostly about the positive, useful, renewal, rebirth, new beginning and reinforcing of life. They are blessings and gifts to humans.

Many people believe that the flowers and bees developed at the same time since they needed each other. Possibly, the beauty in flowers was established as a mechanism to catch the attention and lure pollinators into their direction. The diet of the bees is flower based, taking nectar and pollen from the bulb. Most of the human's diets are flower based. It is all the vegetables, seeds, nuts, and fruits we eat that the bees pollinate. Flowers symbolize and represent the perfect definition of beauty on earth. The fragrances and colors of every type of flowers are natural and sophisticated; hence, can't be reproduced, but could only be

imitated. And that is the source of food for bees.

CHAPTER FIVE

Beekeeping Equipment

As a beekeeper, you must have some necessary tools for honey collection and beehive management. Generally, bees are attracted to dark colors. Hence, the ideal cloth is a light color. Perfumes, colognes and scented lotions also attract bees. So avoid them.

Conventional beekeeping requires some special tools and equipment with a few specific devices to guard against the sting. These tools include the followings:

1. **Smoker**

This is an essential tool for keeping bees. It's a metal container with attaching bellows. A smoker is used to blow a puff of smoke on the hives when the need arises.

2. Beekeeping Brush.

A very soft hairbrush is usually recommended to be used by beekeepers for removing bees from the hive to avoid cell damage. Horsehair is the most common.

3. Scraper/Hive Tool.

This tool very handy for loosen hive parts, scraping wax and manipulating frames. Hive tool or scraper is a popular tool for keeping bees.

4. Knife or Wax Cutter

You will need either electrical or regular wax cutters, to cut the capping of cells to turn honey. An electric knife is more helpful but, an uncapping roller, fork or sharp knife can be used as well.

5. Wax heating pot

For you to make a wax sheet, you will need to melt the wax. The wax sheet can be made or purchased at beekeeping stores.

6. Wax sheet maker

This tool is used to make a bee frame foundation that will help bees in building their nest with ease. Wax foundation aids their performance in using wax to make their nest.

7. Comb puller

Bee comb is usually fastened with propolis. Hence it becomes challenging to be removed with a bare hand. Using comb puller makes the task of removing comb easy, even sticky combs.

8. Beehive Equipment

Hives can be ordered online or purchased from other beekeepers and local dealers. Hives are, without any doubt, a vital tool for the beekeepers. All the components and devices such as nails, foundation pins, boxes and boards with starter kits must be assembled to build beehives. You can buy these tools as they are to be assembled compared with home-made tools. The various parts of your hives are top and bottoms bars, net trap, entrance hole, outer cover, inner cover, brood chamber, and so on.

Since it's important to check your hives at a regular interval, you may need to run-through assembling and disassembling the hives before starting your beekeeping.

Beehive Frames and Feeder

After acquiring your bees and installing your beehives, install a honeybee feeder in your hive to feed the bees if nectar is not available. Put one feeder at the entrance of the hive and another on the edge of the direct brood chamber, a 3rd pail feeder on the inner cover hole and the 4th baggy feeder on the planks alongside the top bars, while you place the 5th frame feeder alongside the frames in the upper deep hive.

Install Beehives and Feeder. For the first few weeks of beekeeping, the feeder is a significant portion of the hive. Bear in mind, all of the options for feeder installment might not be available in all hive arrangement. Only one feeder is needed for a single hive structure.

A beehive includes the following parts:

i. **Frames super box**. You will place 10 frames super box on the top of 10 frames brood chamber.

ii. **Brood chamber/box**. This is the bottom part of beehives. It can be eight or ten frames.

iii. **Super box**. In the season of harvesting, the super box is kept on top the brood chamber. The frames of the super box should equal or lesser than brood box in numbers.

iv. **Top cover**. After the installation of the hive, you will cover with a top coat to prevent wind and rain. The bees will fasten with propolis acquired from trees to hold tight with the body. They will also enclose with wax if there is slight space or hole in the frame.

v. **A separator between brood and super box** The separator is being used to put apart the queen from laid eggs in the super box when harvesting. Super box is installed for honey harvest. If eggs are being laid on it by the queen, it's hard to remove for harvesting and may eventually get damaged.

vi. **Eight or ten frames with a wax sheet** (prepared by bees or manually attached) In general, two types of boxes can be used eight or ten frames. Wax sheet refers to the synthetic beehive created by beekeepers with wax for the bees to aid the completion of their natural hive.

vii. **A feeder pot to feed manually in offseason**. This is typically used only in the off-season when there is a shortage of nectar or flowers. Sugar syrup will be kept in feeder pot daily by beekeepers as an alternative feed.

9. Beekeeping Suit and Veil

Beekeeping suit is a cloth that covers the body, usually made of light-colored materials. To protect your face and body from bee's sting, you need to wear a beekeeping suit and veil. They are protective devices and very important for beekeeping, particularly for the beginners. You should also wear covered shoes and gloves. Remember, bees can crawl up and penetrate your cloth. Thus, use string or masking tape to cover any openings. However, with time, you can wear ordinary cloth in place of beekeeping suit, but as a beginner, wear a high-quality mask to protect your neck, body, face, and eyes

Beekeeping suits include:

i. **Beekeepers veil**: This will protect the face, shoulder, neck, and head from bee's sting.

ii. **Full shirt and pant**: These will protect the entire body from bees sting. Ensure there is no space between the cloth and your body to guarantee complete safety.

iii. **Safety shoes:** Safety shoe will also protect your legs from bee's sting and make you smart enough for handling beehives. Always allow your pant end to be inside the safety shoes.

iv. **Hand Gloves**: Gloves will keep your hand safe in the process of working on beehive Leather hand gloves are ideal for achieving the best result.

10. Spinning equipment or Honey extractor

i. **Honey Extractor or Manual Harvester**: If you have a few beehives, you can extract honey manually. It is therefore suggested for part-time beekeepers.

ii. **Automatic Honey Extractor**: This is recommended for professional beekeepers or those with large bee farm. It is almost impossible to extract honey manually when keeping numerous or thousands of beehives

iii. **Sugar Syrup making pot**: In dry season when natural flowers are not available for bees to obtain sufficient nectar for their feeding, sugar syrup can be made as an alternative to nectar to keep your bees alive and healthy.

iv. **Sieve or filter to clean syrup or honey**: When extracting honey or filtering sugar syrup, a filter is needed to get rid of all clutters from syrup or honey.

In the process of extracting honey, a high number of dead bees and wax are being muddled with honey. Therefore, to separate them, you will need to filter it thoroughly.

v. **Funnel/cone**. This is used to quickly and conveniently fill up a bucket or jar with honey.

11. Honey (Manual) Processing Equipment

i. **Heater**: A heater with control switch is essential for manual processing

ii. **Pots and wooden separators**. These separators are being used to separate two containers or prevent direct heat that could spoil some honey ingredients.

iii. **Temperature indicator or thermometer**: This is being used to control heat level (to avoid excessive heat) while adopting the manual processing method,

iv.   **Moisture indicator**. This is being used to check honey thickness and moisture or to maintain a moderate level of honey moisture. The average moisture range is between eighteen to twenty-two percent

The above 4 equipment is essential for manual processing.

12. Honey (Automatic) Processing Machine

This is only suggested for the commercial beekeepers because it's very costly. However, a small power blanket can be used as an alternative. It is cheap and straightforward.

CHAPTER SIX

Deciding Where to Put Your Beehive

If you are planning to become a professional beekeeper and honey producer, it is imperative to consider where to situate your beehives. Managing many hives doesn't demand massive investment in space and time. All it requires to make your beekeeping activity successful are brilliant decisions. Here are 5 essential factors to consider when deciding where to place your hive:

- Wind direction

- Neighbors

- Sun exposure

- Dampness

- Access to water

Honeybees can be raised in different locations. All you need to do is look for a perfect site for your bees within your environment. Cities, rural landscapes, suburbs can offer a suitable settlement for beehives. Finding an ideal location shouldn't be a problem for you as a new beekeeper. Find out what is allowed and needed in your environment. Make a logical analysis of all your options before quitting.

Some groups of beekeepers develop communal bee yards allowing members to actualize their dreams of owning hives, even if they don't have an ideal location in their house.

Select an area that would not obstruct daily life. Calm and easy to keep honey bees can sometimes turn defensive and testy. A beehive having sixty-thousand bees is not ideal to be right at your back door.

Beehives are hefty. Though they can be moved, it's much better not to move them. Your family members or neighbors might not derive the same pleasure you enjoy with the bees. Some municipal beekeepers have hives on rooftops of their houses. However, there are many other alternatives.

Hives could be situated inside fenced gardens. With this, the human walking path would have been separated from the colony flight path. So the residents wouldn't be scared of functioning beehives situated in their neighborhood

Some beekeepers plant a line of scrubs on three wings of their bee yard. Some choose outside privacy screens which the required maintenance is less than a living shrub.

Meanwhile, there is likelihood for a shrub to catch a bee swarm if one leaves your hive. You can also use artificial shrub.

The rural dwellers have more options. Choosing where to place your beehive is not a problem with much available open space. Contact your local authorities before investing in beekeeping as some communities don't support honey beehive.

If you have other beekeepers in your community, they could be of great assistance for you to choose a better location.

Begin with a few hives. Beekeepers that invest in a large number of hives from the start encounter more difficulties. A beekeeper with a lot of beehives in a location would benefit when having a broader space to utilize.

You don't necessarily need to place your beehives close to a field of wildflowers. Most beginners worry about what bees will be feeding on, as they live in a heavily woody location or city with few blooms. That should not be a problem. Honey bees would fly as far as possible to search for nectar, pollen, and water. Though the closer these resources are to the hives, the more prolific your colony will be.

You can plant flowers that assist bees and other pollinators. Connecting with nature and understanding the balance is an Integra part of beekeeping. You may plant bulbs that bloom when there are no available natural nectar sources.

Place Your Beehives on a Stand

You need to keep your beehives off the ground for easier lifting. You can construct strong wooden stands and place on them. Keep in mind if it works well, your hive will have above one or two boxes. Would you be fit to lift fifty to seventy-five pounds boxes off the top in the period of harvest?

You can also place your beehives on cement blocks (16 high), placing a few landscape timbers on the blocks to hold the hives. Whichever technique will work but ensure your stand is strong enough to hold more than a few pounds.

An ordinary plastic hive stand could work perfectly for some beekeepers as they are strong enough to hold the hive and can be easily relocated if need be. Above all, they do uplift the beehive above the ground. This will prevent your beekeeping tools from moistures from the ground.

How many bee colonies can you have in one location?

The number of bee colonies you can have depends on the foraging and climatic conditions. Consult beekeepers in your locality and be realistic in you set goals. A location that could feed fifty hives during the blooms may find it challenging to feed twenty colonies in a bad nectar year. This is a different perspective of honey bee management.

Also, take bee health and management task into consideration. Safety for you, people and bees must also be considered. Even within your yard, some locations would be better than others.

If you try to work most of the guidelines in your location, life will be more comfortable for you and the bees. Taking into account the following ideas will also help you learn where you cannot put your beehive:

Accessibility to the Bees

Position your colonies in a place you can easily reach in every season without the obstruction of snow, mud etc. As you carry out checks and maintenance all through the year. If there is need to feed your bees, you will need to use a cart or drive a vehicle to move a couple of gallons of sugar water and equipment to the hive, as the more the hives, the more the required feed. If there is a need to shift a bee colony with heavyweight, will you be able to reach easily? Even in snowy and muddy climate.

Beehive Placement and Predators

It is crucial to protect your beehives by constructing a fence. The concern is not only about animal predators. There are human predators too, from to time we hear of beekeepers complaining of their stolen beehives. When deciding where to place your beehives, consider a very close location that would be easier for you to guard. If your colony is to be situated in a far distance, it is advisable not to disclose the area to the people.

Place Your Beehives in the Right Direction

The directions which will you position your beehive is also essential. Take your time to weigh all the available options before you place your hive. A location with full sun is ideal. Most beekeeping guidelines recommended that beehives should be positioned with the entrance facing the eastern or southeastern direction from your area. So the front of the hive can receive early morning sunlight to keep the bees warm and active for the day. It boosts the bee's moral to start the day with passion and begin to work. If this suggestion is not suitable for your location, you do not need to get too hung up on it. However, do not place making the entrance of the beehives facing cold winter wind direction.

Hives Need Good Ventilation

Ventilation is another essential factor to put into consideration when placing beehives. Bees living in a location with excessive humidity are predisposed to diseases. If the site is too close to a source of water, the bees are at the risk of flooding. Keep in mind that bees do not necessarily have to be right close to the stream as they can fly. It is ideal for the bees to have quick access to water. Situate the beehives out of the floodplain but a location with an excellent air-flow.

Consider the Need for a Windbreak

Where is the best to place your beehive if you reside in an environment with the full wind? If you are living in a cold, windy climate, try to protect your colonies against wind. A windbreak could be an erection of a living wall of greenery or ordinary fence.

Shade or Sun Consideration:

Which is the best location for beehives shade or full sun? If you do not reside in an environment with small hive beetles, speckled sunlight is the ideal location for your beehives. Locating beehives in hot sun makes the bees more active. However, small hive beetles appear to like hives sited in the shade. Situating your colony in a location with the full sun may help in preventing beetles. If your only option is the shaded area, you have to be more proactive in beetle activities.

These are tips on where best to place your beehives, don't wait till you have a perfect location. Consider all the guidelines and pick the best among your available spaces.

CHAPTER SEVEN

How to Acquire Your Own Bees

Purchase bee

You can purchase bees, lure a swarm, or catch swarms or to your beehives. The fastest and most steadfast means to acquire bees as a beginner is to purchase. Bees can be bought from a fellow backyard beekeeper, ordered from a supplier or a retailer.

Suppliers are beekeepers that raise bees and queens to sell. They sell the bees in packages or nuc. A package is a screen box with caged queen and un-caged bees, while a nuc is a five-frame hive. A nuc is preferable since bees are already making use of frames in the box, which could be easily transferred directly into your beehive without upsetting the bees. The queen is already integrated into the colony and even started laying eggs. This raises the likelihood of the bees residing in your hive. The queen in packaged bees will be new to the colony and bees would be shaken into their new beehives. The queen and the bees are more probable to fly away if there is nothing to encourage them remains in your hive, Suppliers usually sell bees during the spring, and you might need to pre-order yours as early as the preceding autumn.

Retailers are those that sell other beekeeping equipment and bees. They serve as dealers for suppliers. They take pre-orders, handling sales and deliveries. Understand that the bees available for purchase, (except marketed or else) are possible to have been taken care of with chemicals to eradicate mites and prevent other diseases and parasite. You are required to maintain these bees' treatment to keep alive and healthy. Otherwise, the colony will not function well.

Backyard beekeepers may occasionally need to reduce the number of their beehives or want to quit the business entirely. You can purchase bees from them at any period of the year, and when you are buying from them, you are to get the complete hive, not merely a package or nuc. But remember that used tools and accessories could be a route for parasites and diseases. Investigate the condition of the bee yard or apiary from which you want to purchase your bees. How healthy is the colony? It is advisable to bring along a proficient beekeeper to help you evaluate the well-being of the apiary before buying. Nevertheless, try to purchase your bees from a location that its climatic condition is similar to yours. With this, you will be less concern about the bees adapting to your beehives environment. And it adds to their chances of survival.

1. Catching Swarms

Catching swarms is a different means of acquiring bees. You can get on the swarm list of your locality via the state beekeeping association or local beekeeping club. You can as well create awareness to the local emergency board that you are ready to take away swarms. Swarms are usually made of a matured queen and several worker bees. There is every possibility that they will have mites in their midst, so handle them carefully when housing them. It could be hard to maintain a swarm if you have only new tools. Possibly you add a honey frame in the box to encourage them reside. You can purchase this from a beekeeper in your locality, but freeze it for about twenty-four hours before using it. To get rid of any parasites that might remain from the former colony.

2. Lure Bees

Luring bees to your newly acquired beehives could be challenging. If you possess a few old beekeeping tools, roving scout bees may locate it and persuade their associates to choose the colony as their new abode. If all your equipment is brand new, you can add some drops of lemon-grass essential oil on the frame and in the box. Bees are quite attracted to the smell. This proved effective; you can try it. Remember, no matter where the fragrance is located, the aroma will entice them. Be mindful of how to handle the essential oil, so the bees don't turn hostile.

Getting started with beekeeping could be costly when purchasing bees and acquiring bee tools and accessories. However, if you are planning to capture your bees, you could save yourself some expenses.

CHAPTER EIGHT

Feeding Honeybees

Wondering how your honey bees are not going to be starved or whether there are sufficient stores to survive all through the winter. Also, you may make it a responsibility by encouraging your colony to build up well during the spring for sound health. The question of when and how to feed them now arise?

Ideally, if you leave sufficient honey for the bees, the need for feeding them may not be necessary. Nevertheless, in a situation where there is a reduced flow of nectar, and also the bees don't have sufficient honey stored, especially when you start a new colony in the spring. If you could easily pick up your hive, it may be light on honey. A respective colony needs a minimum of about fifty to sixty pounds of stored honey to prevent them from being starved during the winter.

For honeybees to continually supply you with honey, they need to be fed, especially in bad years. The below tips are mainly based on the National Bee Unit guide to feeding bees, which includes pollen, water, and sugar feeding.

Feeding them their own honey is more preferred to refined sugar. Keep sufficient honey for the bees that could last them for the year.

Make sure there are sufficient pollen-bearing plants close to the hives for you to guarantee adequate pollen for the bees all through the year.

Make sure there is access to a clean water supply for the bees

Other Tips includes:

- Avoid leaving syrup open to the bees or spilling in the apiary

- Maintain proper care to stay away from robbing

- Ensure your hive is level and all the syrups are made available to the bees

When to Feed

The moment there is little or no flow of nectar and a colony is short of stores. This can be experienced in the time of the year when you have two combined hives or when you have a swarm.

Honeybees stock honey in the hive to make food available in winter and other periods when nectar-secreting flowers are scarce. When there is unavailability or shortage of nectar, they rely on their honey stored in the hive. Through these periods, it's vital to monitor the amount of honey in the hive often because when it has all gone, the colony will starve.

Honey as feed for bees

Don't feed bees with honey except it is from your own hygienic beehives. American foulbrood disease may be in honey. To feed them from an unfamiliar supply, for example, another beekeeper or supermarket might lead to infection in your beehives. Feeding your bees with good honey, it must be placed inside the hive. Don't place honey in the open outside the hive as this is illegal under the Livestock Disease Control Act 1994.

How to Feed Bees

A variety of feeders can be used to feed your bees, but ensure the type you select is in line with the needs of your bees and the climatic condition. A hive-top feeder built from an inverted with several small holes in the middle of the cover, work well. Also, mason jars could be inverted in the same way.

When feeding or checking on the bees during winter, don't open the hive except the outside is at least forty-degree F with little or no wind. At no time should you remove frames to inspect them, except the outside is nothing less than sixty degree F.

When feeding bees, you need to consider whether you wish to encourage the production of brood or not. Some feed stimulates brood production than others. Granulated sugar, for example, does not promote brood production due to its low water content. You can feed as much as necessary. Excessive feeding can result in bees swarming or overproduction of brood.

If you have stored enough honey, let your bees feed on it. The best food for bees is honey produced from your bees. From time to time, beekeepers reserve the dark-colored or other off-honey for the bees to feed on in an emergency. If not, feed dry sugar or make sugar syrups.

Pollen Patties

You can also feed bees with pollen patties if necessary as they need protein. You can purchase or make it from dry powder. Put the pollen patty on the top bars. Feed pollen patties in early spring as it is crucial for early spring brood rearing □

Fondant and Sugar Candy

You can also feed bees with fondant and sugar candy in the winter in case of emergency and if it's too cold for sugar syrup.

How to Prepare Sugar candy: Add twelve pounds of sugar to a quart of boiling water, stir thoroughly, and allow simmering for about fifteen minutes, and then add ½ tsp of cream of tartar. Allow it cool, mix thoroughly and pour into the feeder. Once cooled, invert the feeder above the frames holding the cluster.

How to Prepare Fondant: Boil a quart of water in a large pot, turn off the heat, add five lb. granulated sugar and stir thoroughly. Allow the sugar to dissolve. Boil the water the second time and keep stirring until the mixture turns hard to about 260° to 270° F on a candy thermometer. Pour into cookie sheets or molds lined with wax paper. Allow to cool, and break into smaller piece, place in wax paper and store in the freezer.

If dry sugar or sugar syrup is given in the open, it will attract bees from nearby colonies and will result in feeding other bees together with your own. The positioning of sugar syrup or dry sugar in hives is to be done around the evening period to reduce the possibility for bees robbing the hives that are fed.

Making and feeding sugar syrup

There are contrary views concerning the amount of sugar in a syrup. Some beekeepers favors a proportion of one portion water to one portion sugar, measured by weight 1:1. Others support thick syrup of one portion of water to two parts of sugar (known as 1:2). In general, 1:1 syrup is used as a supplement to honey stored, to promote comb foundation, drawing and stimulating colonies to rear brood, especially during spring. The other syrup is used to supply food when there no sufficient honey stored in the hive. Measuring the water and sugar by volume or weight is appropriate as it must be a hundred percent sugar concentrations.

Instruction

- Boil the water in a large pot that can sufficiently hold both sugar and water.

- Once the water is boiled, carefully take the pot out of its source of heat.

- Pour the sugar into the boiled water and stir the mixture thoroughly until the sugar dissolved.

- Do not boil the mixture as the sugar might caramelize, partially toxic and indigestible to bees.

- Always allow the syrup to be cooled to the level of room temperature before feeding bees with it.

- You can give cooled syrup to the bees using any of the following methods:

I. Container with a sealable cover

Fill up a clean tin or jar with a sealable lid or any container with a similar feature with sugar syrup.

- Punch or drill the cover with six to eight thinning holes.

- Cut 2 pieces of wood (twelve mm high risers) and position them crosswise the crown bars of the frame in the top box of the hive.

- Upturn the filled-up jar and put it on the risers.

- Position an empty super on the hive to cover the feeder and replace the hive cover. The risers give bees room between the holes and top bars in the container cover.

- Remember to take out the cardboard insertion usually found in the container lids.

II. Plastic bag

- Fill a plastic freezer bag half-way with sugar syrup.

- Softly squeeze the bag to release the air.

- Tie the bag neck with a flexible rope.

- Put the tied bag on top bars of the frames in the top box of hive underneath the cover of the hive. ☐☐

- Make about six to eight thinning holes into the upper surface of the bag using a small diameter nail or brad. It's from these holes the bees will suck the syrup.

- Do not make the holes on the bottom surface of the bag as it might cause rapid leaking out of the syrup. This can result in a shortage of syrup from the outer of hive and result in robbing close by bees.

- Leave space between the base of the hive cover an upper surface of the bag for the bees to have access to syrup.

- You can use a wooden riser of the hive length to raise the lid, if necessary.

III. **Shallow tray**

- Put sugar syrup in a shallow tray-like foil underneath the beehive cover.

- Place some wood or grass straw (the type used in cooling devices) inside the syrup to prevent the bees from drowning or falling into the liquid while trying to reach the syrup.

- Keep in mind not to use straw or floating that has been in contact or been treated with chemicals, as this might be unsafe to the bees.

- You may need to use a riser if the tray is not shallow.

IV.   Frame feeder

- Put sugar syrup in a division or frame board feeder. This is a bowl, the size of a full-depth Lang troth frame, which sits in the super like a standard frame with an open top.

- The feeder needs a floating material or other stuff to give bees' access to the syrup without drowning.

How Often to Feed Bees

Habitually, bees will remove the syrup from a feeder. Reduce the content of the water and store in the combs like honey. Whichever feeder is used, an average to a full colony will typically empty it in a matter of days. For colony with nearly no available nectar and no stored honey, the first feed would be mostly determined by the size of the colony, the number of brood and to some extent, the size of the container filled with the syrup. You can supply a colony with excess than to stint and bring about the colony's death. Some new beekeepers have tried tbsp of syrup, but this is a lesser amount. An initial feed of about one to three liters can be tried. You then need to regularly check the combs to see the amount of syrup that has been stored. It will serve as a guideline as to how much and how often syrup should be given. You can stop feeding when nectar becomes available.

A well-ripened syrup should at least have eighteen percent of moist content. Unripe syrup would ferment and severely affect bees. Colonies without sufficient stores for winter should be supplied with syrup necessary to augment their stores before the cold climate of autumn begins. This would allow the bees to process the syrup adequately.

Feeding dry sugar

An Average to a full colony could be fed dry white table sugar put on trays or beehive mats beneath the hive cover. Bees need water to dissolve the sugar crystals. They could sometimes make use of condensation that may occur inside the hive or get from a source outside the hive. Some beekeepers may choose to wet the sugar with water to stop it from being solid. This produces partial syrup. Irrespective of the size of the colony, dry sugar feeding works well in the autumn and spring when humidity is at its peak. The bees find it difficult to dissolve sugar crystal into liquid in the dry, hot the summer.

Preferably at starvation level, a colony could be first fed syrup before given dry sugar. With this, bees would have been given food directly without the need to dissolve crystals. Usually, when bees can gather enough nectar to the colony, they would not make use of dry sugar. The sugar will be sometimes deposited outside the hive entrance by the bees. They may convert a small amount the dry sugar to fluid and stored in the cells

Note:

Do not extract the remaining sugar in combs with the next honey produce, as this will pollute the honey, and the extracted harvest will not be in conformity with the honey established legal stand. Typically, in the period of the honey flow, the bees would consume the entire sugar that is supplied to the hives. Also in the time of brood nest expansion, bees would move the sugar stored in the brood nest combs to the honey super.

Bees feeding in spring: Feed thin sugar syrup when bees have a shortage of stores in the spring inspection.

Bees feeding in summer: Feed thin sugar syrup when bees have a shortage of stores in the summer.

Bees feeding in autumn: If in late July or early August you harvest your honey, this will allow the bees to store their own honey for the winter period. The period of the year to feed thick sugar syrup is September to early October, to ensure enough stores for the bees throughout the winter. Do the feeding after you must have removed the honey crop and the colony is still healthy, adequately warm for bees to move up to the feeder, capable of taking down the syrup, invert and store in the comb properly. Early feeding will most likely change to broods, so except there is a threat of hunger, postpone till September. An average honeybee colony needs around twenty kilograms of stores. A full standard British brood frame contains two and a half kilogram of honey, hence the need to check the existing colony stores and supply the needed balance with sugar syrup. A frame of 14×12 is made of approx. 3.75 kilograms. Note: 1Kg of sugar will create 1.25Kg of stores in the brood box.

Bees Feeding In Winter: If there is a shortage of stores during the winter and there is the possibility that bees will be starved, place bee candy on top of the crown board feed holes. You may need to turn the crown board, to put a feed hole above the bee cluster. Bees need water regularly used as condensation within the hive to utilize candy.

Emergency Feeding: In a situation where bees are starving, feed them with thin sugar syrup solution and fill up a vacant comb with sugar syrup content. You can do this by carefully pouring the syrup into the cells with a squeezes bottle. Position the comb next to the bees when filled.

Feeding Pollen

The best way to provide sufficient pollen for bees is to make sure there are enough pollen carrier plants in the bees surrounding. You can feed pollen substitute, pollen gathered in the previous season or pollen patty, if there are no sufficient pollen stores. Bee diseases can be spread, hence ensure to collect only from a strong and disease-free colony making use of a good pollen trap. ☐

Don't leave the trap on the hive at all time as this could reduce the pollen with time. Avoid gathering pollen in time of major honey flows. You can feed about 50 hives adequately with pollen collected from one hive. And avoid feeding with other beekeeper's pollen.

The most convenient method of storing pollen is to put it in plastic bags or paper and store in a freezer at 18°C. Use it immediately when defrosted. You can feed a colony with fresh liquefied pollen by putting it in a shallow bowl near the feed hole. You can purchase a pollen substitute from a certified commercial supplier. Ensure you follow the supplier's recommendation when feeding substitutes

Feeding Water

If there are no natural water sources, you can purchase a water feeder from equipment suppliers to supply bees with water. Keep in mind, when preparing your feeder that it's natural for the bees to suck up moistness from a damp surface like brick, sand, or soil rather than from an exposed surface of water. An area with approx 75cm^2 for each colony is needed. Don't allow the moisture to be stagnant. The watering area should be smaller than the landing area. Bees prefer water that is warmer than 18°c. Combine a little salt to inspire the bees to take the water when giving for the first time.

Feeding and Robbing

Here are the tips to prevent robbing:

- Reduce entrance to the hive with an entrance block.

- Best time to feed is in the evening.

- Look out for signs of robbing (bees fighting and struggling to go into a hive without meeting the guards) If you notice this, minimize bee's entrance to one bee space with grass or an entrance block. This allows guard bees to be more effective in protecting the colony.

- You can also move the affected colony to another apiary

CHAPTER NINE

Inspecting Beehive

1. Get Ready to Open the Hive.

Inspection of your beehive must be done regularly. Every 7 -10 days in the spring and summer is ideal for beginners. Your bees will not be pleased if your inspection is more than weekly. Keep in mind that each time you inspect, it interrupts their hive activities and pulls them a day back.

Firstly, you will assemble your beekeeping equipment: hive tools, smoker and if you would be refilling feeders in the course of the inspection, prepare them for a refill. You will wear your bee jacket or suit and veil. You will also ignite your smoker and pumping out cold, pleasant smoke for the bees.

2. Open the Hive

The opening of the outer lid, your tools are at your disposal, and you are ready to uncover your beehive. Place smoke directly in front of the hive entrance to obscure the guard bees. After that, crack the outside lid and direct a couple of smoke puffs beneath it. Put down the lid back gently and pause for a few minutes for the smoke to come into effect.

People believe that smoke "calms" the bees, but in real sense, it passes signals to them that fire is close by, and thus enables them to gorge on honey. During their gorging on honey, they would not be worried about you in white-suit messing with them. When you see them staring at you with their small heads team up at the top bars, that's the moment for a further smoke.

3. Remove Outer Cover

After you must have waited for the smoke to calm them a little, take out the outer lid and cautiously put it upside-down on the floor. You can now direct a couple of puffs of smoke into the hole in the inner cover and wait for few minutes for the bees to receive the signal.

4. Remove Inner Cover

Having removed the outer cover and puffed the smoke in the direction of the central cover hole, make use of your hive equipment to lift the interior lid and take it out softly. If there is propolis or wax on the inside cover, scratch it off with your hive equipment. Carefully place the inner cover above the outside cover on the floor.

5. Remove the Super

Remove the honey super with your hive equipment and gently place on the inside cover.

6. Smoke the Deep Hive Box

Now you need to softly puff some smoke into the second deep or hive box, and if you have 3 medium boxes rather than 2 deeps, you would repeat the same process until you reach the last box and then begin your inspection with the last box.

7. Remove the Second Deep.

Remove the second deep and softly place it on top of the inside cover or super and inspect it later.

8. Smoke Bees and Takeout First Frame

Puff the smoke in the direction of the frames in the last deep hive box. Take out the first frame and gently place it either on top of the inside cover or the other hive boxes or in a frame holder. Be careful as you do so to avoid smashing bees.

9. Inspect Frames

Use your hive tools to check each frame with care. Hold it up and inspect the frame. Look for brood, eggs, capped and uncapped larvae. See if you could recognize the queen (easy to identify if marked), you will look for a group of workers surrounding her and her lengthy, slim un-stripped abdomen. If you are unable to find the queen, try to locate eggs to confirm the queen was there within one to three days ago.

Check for any pests or parasites – foulbrood, wax moth larvae, and mites and so on. Check the number of frames that are drawn out. If the numbers are up to seven to ten in the bottom deep, you will need to add the second one. If in the second deep, seven to ten frames are drawn out, add a honey super. When a particular honey super is almost full, you can add another one.

10.   Check for Larvae

This is the right way of rising uncapped larvae to demonstrate to you what you're searching for in your hive examination.

11. Find Honeybee Eggs

The most significant aspect of the beehive inspection for the beginners is to recognize honeybee eggs. However, most beginners find it too hard to identify eggs. Here are some tips to have an idea of what eggs seem like in the cells:

- Eggs are like thin grains of rice. You will see one egg laid in the center of each cell. If you see more than one egg in a cell, those are laying workers – contact a proficient beekeeper about this condition.

- The best means of seeing eggs is to hold the frame at an angle, neither horizontal nor vertical but tilted up about thirty-degree angles in the sky direction.

- Slightly hold it to your side not right in front of you, so the shadow form of your veil net does not block your view of the eggs.

- You can use magnifying glasses or reading glasses to help in viewing.

- You can also look in the direction of the bottom center of the frame for quick eggs identification.

12.   Replace the Frames

After inspecting each frame, place it into open space left by the first frame you removed. Softly thrust every single frame to the one in front of it as you swap it, to avoid crushing any bees. Making use of a smoke or bee brush to move the bees out of the way, particularly at the area close to the frame where they could be squeezed. Inspect frames orderly and do not alter the order of the frames in the course of the inspection. When you reach the last frame, thrust the entire set of frames simultaneously using your hive equipment as a single unit, creating space in the front for the first frame. Replace it and then make use of your hive equipment to level up space on both sides of the first and last frames so the set of frames will be at the center of the box.

Use the same method for the last/bottom box to inspect and replace the second box too. Having done that, you can now replace the super. Start with the box on the hive back edge. Slowly and carefully slide it forward to avoid squishing bees. Now you can make use of bee brush or smoker to move bees out of the way. Particularly at the end, when you are about to complete the process of sliding the box on.

13.   Replace Interior Cover

Slide the inner cover on, start at one end and carefully slide the cover over the box. Make use of bee brush or smoker to move bees out of the way as required.

14.   Replace Outer Cover

Softly replace the outside cover of the hive. That's all, but it's essential to take a record of your observations in your bee journal or notebook as you can easily forget the details and dates of inspection.

CHAPTER TEN

The Honey Flow

Honey flow period is referred to the time when bees have access to abundant of resources, allowing them to hasten the production of honey within the hive. So, the honey flow is less about the flow of honey and more about bees having regular access to the nectar that would assist them in producing a large amount of honey. The flow of honey happens when most important nectar sources are accessible, alongside right weather to enable bees forage for plenty of nectar. The availability of sufficient honey is the outcome of the honey flow – The period when bees have a great opportunity to produce honey.

When Does the Flow Of Honey Occur?

Good weather is related to the period of the year, and surely, the most supportive of the flow of honey is summer period. However, it's not only in the summer. The flow of honey also occurs in the spring when several flowers bloom.

What Factor Affects the Honey Flow?

Several factors affect when the flow of honey occurs. The two primary requirements are good weather and access to nectar. We have several reasons why the climate may not be friendly, apart from just the temperature. For instance, spring typically comes with breezy conditions not favorable to the flow of honey. So, the climate element of the flow of honey is varied.

The other factors – close nectar access – this could be slightly anticipated based on the kind of available flowers in the locality and their flowering schedules. This is a part that is not supposed to be left only to nature as the beekeepers can considerably influence this with a little preparation.

When to Expect a Substantial Honey Flow:

As a beekeeper, you will experience flow and ebb during the warmer months and bees may be able to produce a large quantity of honey in multiple times. Nature is complex, and there are convoluted connections between the blooming of flowers and weather patterns. Generally, an experienced beekeeper will be able to clarify, with practical experience when to precisely expect the flow of honey.

How to Take Note of the Honey Flow

Since the flow of honey is prompted by the blooming of flowers within miles of the beehive, you can't just examine resident flowers to conclude that the flow of honey has arrived. You can only know by observing your bee's behavior. The most apparent indication is the rate of activities and the number of bees hunting. A set of bees would come back to the hives with abundant nectar, while other groups are preparing to leave for more collection.

The consequential view is pleasing to the beekeepers – bees flowing in and out of their hive in multiples. It is really a sight to see. All these activities are connected to a rapid upsurge in the quantity of honey produced. For this period, you do not have to distract bees with frequent inspections. What is noteworthy is to be aware of the possibility of swarming. In the period of honey flow, there is the possibility of extracting about five lbs of honey in a single hive – just in a day.

What You Can Do to Help

The period of honey flow is not only a time for beekeepers to rejoice, but also a period to be very watchful. The flow of honey signifies a sudden increase in the needed amount of space for the bees within the hive. Any hive with inadequate space could quickly result in a colony with swarming thoughts. A colony that swarms will consequently divide into two and one part will leave the colony for a new home.

A vigilant beekeeper is aware at all times of the space available in the hive. Increasing the beehive by putting additional boxes is a significant choice the beekeeper would consider, given bees extra space for the more honey and hence reducing the possibility of swarming.

Apart from observing visually, the heaviness of the hive is also a significant indicator. Most beekeepers know how to weigh their hives, and the flow is associated with a drastic increase in weight.

Ideally, beekeepers could sow flowers that are purposely selected to blossom in a staggered way all through the season. This will not only add beauty to your garden but also result in an extensive flow of honey as bees fly from a variety of flower to the other for nectar collection.

CHAPTER ELEVEN

Harvesting Honey

It's a great thing to earn the fantastic rewards of beekeeping. Nevertheless, a honey harvest isn't always assured from mere raising bees. The quantity of honey produced by the bees largely depends on the flow of nectar in your area, the kind of bees you keep, the age of your hives and the environmental factors.

Before harvesting, it's imperative to make sure there are sufficient honey stores for bees before winter. Residing in the Northeast, you should fill your deeps with enough honey as the fall is coming to an end. It will serve them all through the months of winter.

In the spring and summer months, place supers on top of the bees, serving as an additional place for the bees to store nectar they would ultimately convert into honey. The honey supers as well offer extra space for the bees to temporarily reside as the colony expands in the months of spring and summer. Once you are prepared for honey harvest, you will need to take out the bees from the honey superframe. You can do this by using several effective methods. You can use a bee brush, leaf blowers or bee escape boards. Keep in mind, remove honey frames only when ninety percent of the comb is capped.

Take your time to remove the bees' one after the other from all the frames full of capped honey. Take each frame to an empty deep positioned under the sun about fifty feet distant from the hive and cover with cloth. It will distance the bees from the frames. These processes could be done on the morning of the honey harvest one or two days before harvesting. Once you have collected every frame, take them to the location where you want to extract the honey.

Some beekeepers extract honey in the garage or kitchen. Remember, wherever your harvesting location is, it should not be accessible to the bees. Always close the doors and windows. Otherwise, bees would perceive the honey harvest and arrive in the nick of time and could turn honey harvesting into a tragedy.

There are several methods you can use to harvest honey from the frames. Using an extractor is the neatest and the fastest. Consult your local bee club for an extractor, as most of the clubs' loans or rents out their extractors. This will help in reducing the expenses.

Once you have extracted the honey, you can leave it in the sealed, five-gallon clean plastic containers or it can be transferred into jars instantly. The jars with their covers should be washed and dried before putting the honey.

If you want to sell your honey, you will need to label it before selling. Include the following detail:

1. Your farm name /your name

2. The name of the product for example wildflower honey

3. Your contact telephone number/ address

4. The net weight of the package

Your local bee club also could provide guidelines to you as regard pricing the honey per pound. Offering your honey for sale is very rewarding and helps to offset expenses of beekeeping. Organic, unpasteurized honey from direct sources has numerous health benefits and consuming it every day could help in controlling seasonal allergies.

CHAPTER TWELVE

About Beeswax

Bee wax is a fantastic natural material with apparently numerous usages. From candle wax to lip balm, and even as non-plastic food storage, bee wax is an environmentally pleasant substance which every household must have.

The beauty of beeswax includes:

- **It is all-natural**

This wax, being a product of honeycomb of the honey bee, is all-natural material directly from the natural world. Honey bees consume pollen and honey to produce the wax. To create one pound of bee wax, it takes around eight pounds of honey

- **Antibacterial**

Similar to honey, bee wax has antibacterial stuff that helps in keeping things hygienic and reducing the risk of contamination. This makes it a usual ingredient in skin treatments, creams and more.

- **Antifungal**

Bee wax is also believed to have antifungal ingredients that prevent yeasts and other fungi growth.

- **Edible**

Bee wax is non-toxic and harmless if consumed; this is one of the reasons it makes a perfect lip balm, though it may not give several nutrients.

- **Better even when burned**

Different from candles produced from other wax, bee wax candle burns cleaner and brighter as they release negative ions which are recognized to help cleanse the air. Bee wax also smells nice when burned without adding any scents or chemicals, as it has a natural scent from the flower, nectar and honey that are found in the honeycomb.

- **Waterproof**

Bee wax has been used all through history as a waterproofing agent and sealant for material such as shoes, tents, and belts. By rubbing bee wax on a surface like canvas or leather and then heating it, the wax seeps into the fibers and stops water from going through.

- **Moisturizing**

Bee wax is a common ingredient in balms, salves, and lotions. It helps lock in moisture, making it useful for treating hair, lips and dry skin.

- **Eco-friendly**

Since bee wax is non-toxic and is directly from bees, it is ecologically friendly and a vital ingredient in a variety of eco-friendly products.

- **Never goes bad**

Bee wax holds a natural potent protective ingredient called propolis that protects it from spoiling. Produced by the bees with the combination of tree resin with pollen and resin flakes, Pollen is used to strengthening and fixing the beehive while defending the hives with an antiseptic barricade –Propolis is a Greek name, and it means "defense of the city". These defensive abilities are so strong that un-spoilt bee wax has been discovered in ancient tombs. This proved the possibility of homemade or commercial bee wax products which contain other ingredients not to be spoilt. This product, having numerous beneficial ingredients, is a harmless and healthy substitute to plastic for storing food. Super bee beeswax wrap makes use of the natural power of bee wax to store and safely protect your foodstuff as an alternative to a plastic wrap. As far as bee wax is water-resistant, it keeps unwanted moisture out of foodstuff while keeping the food's natural moisture in.

Meanwhile, the antifungal and antibacterial properties in it keep germs and bacteria away from it. Unlike chemical-filled plastic, it is safe to have your foodstuff closed to it since it's non-toxic and all-natural. Most people even use bee wax to seal fresh cheeses.

CHAPTER THIRTEEN

Bee's Pests, Predators and Their Preventions

- **Mites**

There are numerous species of mites. Many of them are parasitic while some live on food like cheese, mold or fungi. Among the growing list of familiar mites, the only 2 that are associated with honey bee are tracheal and varroa mites.

Varroa Destructor or Varroa mite

Is an exterior parasite of the honeybee, we can see them with our naked eyes because of their thickness. They feed on the bee's hemolymph; these mites attack both developing stages of bees and adults. In mid-1980, these insects were transported to the United States via bee's importation and now spread all over the world. Adult female mites are only found attached to bees, which spread them between hives. Attached insects penetrate from behind the head or the weaker tissue amid abdominal segments of the bee's hemolymph. Female mites are attracted to a drone brood pheromone's odor but will invade most about to be capped cells. When in brood cell, the female would tunnel down to the larvae's food supply's base to escape exposure. Once the cell is capped, the mother mite will attach to the bees' larvae and start feeding. The mother will lay unfertilized eggs from which male insects would hatch. Every egg laid will be fertile daughter eggs. The hatched adult males would mate with a few sisters before they die. The sister and mother mites leave the brood cell and start the process all over, once the parasitizing bee finally emerge.

Infected bees, if not killed, would be weakened by the mites and will not live long. The damages caused by varroa to the host bees are yet to be completely established. However, the following are the symptoms of varroosis:

- Presence of disease

- Infected capped brood

- Adult bees disfigured

- Death of colony in late summer

- Adult bees not capable of flying

- Bees disposing of affected pupae and larvae

- Symptoms of sacbrood and Foulbrood present

- Adult and larvae bees bearing reddish-brown spots

- Brittle scales or foul odor

Varroa mites have been discovered to activate viral replication or vector viruses in numerous honeybee diseases. Since they feed on the bee's hemolymph, they expose them to infections and also weaken their immune system. If beehives are infested with a harmless virus such as ABPV, and varroa mites are presented to the viruses, it might lead to a deadly infection. Varroa mites are presently capable of exposing honeybees to about fourteen numerous viruses such as Israel Acute Bees Paralysis Virus (IABV), deformed wing virus, Sac Brood Virus (SBV), Kashmir Bee Virus (KBV). Recent researches have recognized the connection between CCD and varroa infestation, but no perfect outcome has been established.

1. Tracheal Mites (Arcarine Disease)

Acarapis woodi or tracheal mites are recognized as the cause of arcarine diseases. Soon after their detection in 1919, the U.S stopped all importation of bees. Hence the honey bee Act of 1922 was passed. The mite was discovered in 1984 in Mexico and since has spread across most of the modern bee world, excluding some African countries and some Pacific island. These tiny mites are found in high levels in the winter and spring. They breed, live, and lay eggs inside the thoracic tracheal or breathing organs of the adult bees. They will hatch larvae, leave the trachea and crawl along the bee's hair to spread to a new host via contact. The mites are attracted to carbon-dioxide releases, which cause the spiracles and sequential to the trachea of bees.

Adult mites pierce the tracheal tissue to eat the hemolymph of the bees from within the tracheal tube. Any infested tracheal tube would be dark and might look crusted and black in some areas, rather than it's naturally clear, light-colored to brownish-yellow appearance. Tracheal mites have been revealed to cause damages to the bee's flight muscles, probably associated with the air constraint that happens when a tracheal tube is full of mites.

Currently, there is no particular cluster of symptoms positively related to a tracheal mite infection, though there are symptoms usually notice in the occurrence of a disease. Mites infected bees could be detected outside the beehive, with a swollen abdomen and often find it difficult to fly. Adult bees might have disjointed wings or show abnormal wing folding. It's significant to take note of that, though these symptoms are connected to an infestation, their absence doesn't mean mites are not present.

Treatment of Tracheal Mites

Mite infestation can be treated with menthol. It was established that the breathing in of hazes by bees helps in drying off the mites. If you are adopting this method, ensure you remove the menthol during the flows of nectar if not, the honey could be contaminated. You can also treat the infection of a tracheal mite by providing a vegetable and sugar shortening patty. When bees feed on the patty, they will receive a coating of oil. The oil serves as a cover-up, making it more difficult for female mites to discover an appropriate host.

A combination of the 2 methods, menthol inhalation and vegetable and sugar shortening patty has been established to be useful for treating or controlling mites.

Pests Insect and Predators

Honeybees are faced with the challenges of numerous insect enemies. Some of the bee's common enemies are flies, ants, spiders, hive beetles, wax moths and more. Though most of these insects often prey upon bees, not all of them affect the well-being of the colony. Other insects prey on other pests that feed on the store or upon the stored product of the hive. Parasitizing and robbing are also characteristic of honey bees' pests, insects and predators. The following are among the three most dangerous and common insect threats:

1. **Wax Moth**

The greater wax moth or galleria melonella L was discovered in the United States in 1806. This moth is believed to have developed along with Asian honeybees, inadvertently make known to the United States when bees were imported. Wax moths are made known to be sometimes beneficial as they can abolish infected varroa comb or other diseases. They could be raised with bee's products and vend for pet food, fishing bait, and some other usages. Classified by a long grey-brown body, the feminine moths lay eggs in the crevices and cracks of the beehive. Feeding on shed exoskeleton of the bee pollen and larvae and hiding from worker bees. A good number of larvae would move to the hive that is close to them and spread the infection. Silk traces are left behind on the comb as the larvae tunnel. Larvae attach themselves to the hive board and roll themselves in a cocoon when ready to pupate. It has been established that in one season they can wipe out a whole hive, especially if you don't pay attention to the hive. The following are the symptoms of a wax moth infestation:

- Silk cocoons attached to wooden frames and boards

- Silk strands scattered over comb

- Tunnels all through brood comb

- Dark specks of excrement present on hive bottom or in silk strands

- Wreckages on hive bottom- moth larvae, silk strands, damaged comb, etc.

Control methods:

Maintaining strong, healthy colonies is the best method of controlling wax moths. The following are the other controlling methods:

- Clear all debris in the bottom of the hive

- As soon as you detect infection, extract supers and store safely

- Store combs in light for twenty-four-hour, the female moth would not be able to lay eggs where light is present

- Store combs in cool places to deter the infestation and impede the existing population's development

- Freeze combs for up to twenty-four hours to destroy any existing eggs

- Disinfect dry combs with a nitrogen mixture and CO_2

- Burn hive frames showing heavy infestation

2. Small Hive Beetle

Small hive beetle (Aethina tumida) is among the recently detected bee pests. It was discovered in 1998 in the United State (U.S), though there is a slight misperception on its arrival. It was believed to only exist in South Africa where it happens to be an insignificant problem. It presents a big problem in North America. Small hive beetle is characterized by fine hairs covering the body, reddish-brown to black color, three legs and an abhorrence to light. The beetle larvae are cream colored with the appearance similar to those of the wax moth. Female beetles lay eggs in crevices and cracks of the hive that cannot be reached by the bees. After 1 to 6 days, the eggs hatch and larvae arise to feed on honey, pollen and bee brood. Having completed the larval stage, they fall to the bottom of the hive, crawl outside the hive and start pupating into the soil within the hive's environment. Adults raise and move into the hive to mate, and the cycle continues.

Small hive beetle increases in humid, hot climatic condition. When inspecting a hive, you could see beetles running through combs to dodge the light. You can also find adults in crevices around the bottom and top boards of the hive. A small number of female beetles existing in a colony could produce an enormous amount of larvae which could eventually overwhelm the colony. Adult beetles can cause honey to ferment and could contaminate honey by excreting in stored honey. Larvae tunnel through brood comb, consuming resources stores as it goes and killing brood. Removed honey supers are the most susceptible to a hive beetle infection as there are a surplus of honey and a small number of bees. The bees abandon the hive, and the queen stops laying eggs in the case of a severe infestation.

Control Methods:

Maintaining healthy colonies is the ideal protection against small hive beetle infestation, though a large number of beetles may still overpower the strongest of the beehives. Some bee's species build structures with propolis to entrap beetles. The following are the other method of controlling beetle:

- Getting rid of beetles found in the honey super immediately.

- Usage of beetle traps inside and the hive's surrounding.

- Reduce the time between extraction of honey and comb removal.

- Cleaning of the hive by thoroughly washing out the fermented honey.

- Storage of honey in a cool, dry place.

- Moving the infected colonies away from other hives and outside the apiary site.

- Pick queens from beetle resistant inherent backgrounds.

- Melt or dispose of wax stores.

- Spray the hive area soil with approved pesticides to eradicate pupating beetles.

- Don't use contaminated tools on clean colonies.

- Allow fire ants and chickens to prey on infected tools.

3. Animal Pests and Predators

Mice, bears, raccoon, badgers, skunks, and humans represent the utmost barriers in honey bee colonies. Including minor pests, but are not limited to livestock, shrews, rats, squirrels, frogs, lizards, birds and more. The harm caused by these pests' ranges from hive product consumption to hive disruption to hive destruction. Evidence of the existence of these pests is typically shown in alterations visible upon inspection. Humans vandalize or steal hives, mice chew equipment, raccoon scatter the hive equipment, and bears tip hives over.

Control methods:

Keeping hives in a location with restricted access or close to residences that are inhabited year-round. Another reasonable means of discouraging most of these animal pests is to have a fenced area with a locked gate.